If you often approach poetry with skepticism, let down your guard. Alfred Nicol is the rare poet you can surrender to without reservation; you're in superb hands. In his deceptively colloquial poems, Nicol's wit creeps up on you and before you know it becomes philosophy (often with a religious theme).

Masquerading as light verse, "Addendum" paints a secular age devoted to Caesar's realm, leaving nothing on the balance sheet to render unto God. The title poem "After the Carnival" likewise alludes to the Gospel of Matthew: Nicol speculates, with a twist, on God's solicitude for us and our own responsibility in turn—all this in seventeen syllables lodged stubbornly in my brain. "Ordinary Time" refers to the numbered weeks between the Christian holidays; here it describes a reprieve from terminal illness.

The collection includes tragedies (like the haunting deaths of children); but—optimistic or the opposite—it's Nicol's brilliant *jeux d'esprit* that do the serious work.

—DEBORAH WARREN, author of *Connoisseurs of Worms*

Alfred Nicol's *After the Carnival* will remind readers that Nicol is not only one of our best poets, but one of our very best storytellers and the contemporary master of the ballad. His language is gorgeous, his imagery striking, and his thinking deeply layered—in short, this is a book to be savored.

—A. M. JUSTER, translator of Petrarch's *Canzoniere*

The poems in Alfred Nicol's *After the Carnival* are replete with felicities. The wealth of such moments bespeaks a virtuosity of the most virtuous, least show-offy sort. To take an example, a bald eagle atop a floodlight pole eyes a stadium "for small game, / unburdened by the emblematic weight / of victory and empire, wealth and fame, / and looking pretty regal just the same." Nor are these poems merely the sum of their highlights: they're beautifully architected, with all the resources of poetry—form, imagery, syntax, rhythm, meditative depth, narrative drive— repeatedly marshaled in the service of a telling point. Nicol is observant, humane, funny—and, as becomes apparent in the book's climactic last section, a person of faith: a faith in which, like that of George Herbert, this non-believer couldn't help but emotionally participate. I can't recommend *After the Carnival* more highly.

—DAN BROWN, author of *Subjects in Poetry*

Alfred Nicol's writing is remarkable both in its verse craft and its versatility. Often set in Canada or coastal New England, his finely etched lyrics and his sometimes harrowing narratives may recall forebears such as Frost and Robinson. But Nicol's voice and vision are his own, assets of an imagination ready to explore the full range of human feelings, from laughter to tears with all the equivocal ones in between. His energetic diction, often dexterously rhymed, memorably conveys what his sharply observant eyes have taken in. Finely attentive to its persons and places, *After the Carnival* is a book that will be read with delight—and returned to, with renewed wonder at so many things done so unassumingly well.

—ROBERT B. SHAW, Emily Dickinson Professor of English Emeritus, Mount Holyoke College

In one of the final poems in *After the Carnival*, Alfred Nicol writes, "All music's owed to love, that wakes the senses". Love, along with the music love creates, permeates this remarkable collection, although the love exhibited can be tough, surprising, and even, at times, shocking. The poet's eye for the precisely right detail is everywhere evident, whether in poems about Nature—as in his delightful sequence about birds, "Avatars of Appetite"—or those about human interactions, personal, social, and religious. The book abounds with good humor and wit (the title poem, "After the Carnival," for instance, is a haiku, and "Wretched Rocco," about a cat, is hilarious), but is also haunted by darkness, literal as well as existential: "A Notion" ends with "—I wonder, will the spirit absently / recall the flesh that housed it for a time?" "An Irreverent Portrait of Father McLaughlin" is a marvel! These are poems to return to, and to treasure.

—BRUCE BENNETT, author of *Just Another Day in Just Our Town*

In our age of detachment and ironic distance, Alfred Nicol isn't afraid to engage the reader's emotions in poems that range from warm-hearted to marrow-chilling. *After the Carnival* is unified by Nicol's wit, his profound connection to place, and his mastery of poetic craft—but most of all by his empathy and willingness to take emotional risks. Whether examining the "emptiness in everything, / like the shade cradled in the crescent moon" or celebrating the survival of three ants in "a piece of kettle corn / the sparrow lets fall," these poems dig deep, unearthing the sacred and sustaining in a seemingly indifferent universe.

—APRIL LINDNER, author of *This Bed Our Bodies Shaped*

# AFTER THE CARNIVAL

# AFTER THE CARNIVAL

*poems*

*Alfred Nicol*

Wiseblood Books

Copyright © 2025 by Wiseblood Books

All rights reserved, including the right to reproduce this book or any portions thereof in any form whatsoever except for brief quotations in book reviews. For information, address the publisher:

>WISEBLOOD BOOKS
>*Joshua Hren, Editor-in-Chief*
>Post Office Box 870
>Menomonee Falls, WI 53052
>www.wisebloodbooks.com

Cover design: Amanda Brown

Art: *The Burial of the Sardine* by Francisco Goya

Printed in the United States of America
Set in Calluna Type 11.5

ISBN: 978-1-951319-02-1

*For my sons Paul and John*

# Contents

### I. All the World There Is

| | |
|---|---|
| The Path | 3 |
| The Berkshires | 4 |
| A Notable Catch in a Tourist Town | 5 |
| After the Carnival | 7 |
| Blizzard | 8 |
| Canuck Haiku | 9 |
| Stay at Home Advisory | 11 |

### II. The Man in the Middle

| | |
|---|---|
| Addendum | 15 |
| The Man in the Middle | 16 |
| Epigram for Two Voices | 19 |
| Napoleon's Sword | 20 |
| An Indelicate Proposal | 21 |
| Samuel Clemens | 22 |
| Nuclear Option | 23 |

### III. Avatars of Appetite

| | |
|---|---|
| Altogether Alive | 27 |

### IV. Playthings

| | |
|---|---|
| Ballad of the Terrible Silence | 33 |
| The Pastime | 37 |
| Ballad of the Dapper Black Man | 40 |
| The Ghost in the Cathedral | 44 |

## V. A Sheet of Steel, a Blanket of Moss

| | |
|---|---|
| Ordinary Time | 47 |
| Poemmakers | 50 |
| Merry-go-round | 51 |
| House Hunters International | 52 |
| The Surface | 54 |
| Archipelago of Syllables | 55 |
| The Workshop | 58 |
| A Notion | 59 |

## VI. Old Brick Church

| | |
|---|---|
| Tell You the Story | 63 |
| An Irreverent Portrait of Father McLaughlin | 67 |
| Wretched Rocco | 70 |
| His Eyes Rest on Julia, Sleeping | 73 |
| Talking All Night | 74 |
| Gibbous Moon | 77 |
| | |
| Acknowledgments | 79 |
| About the Poet | 81 |

# I

*All the World There Is*

## The Path

It's not a path that takes you very far.
It starts across the field from where you're standing
but only brings you back to where you are.

You try it, like a door that's left ajar.
A little uphill climb, not too demanding;
it's not a path that takes you very far.

It's better, though, than sitting in the car.
The view, while not what you would call "commanding,"
at least gives you a sense of where you are.

Between two pines you glimpse the reservoir
where swallows briefly rest before disbanding.
Their paths, like yours, don't take them very far.

The catbird practicing its repertoire,
the squirrel perched above you, reprimanding,
return you to the sense that, where you are—

though not a garden painted by Renoir—
the monarch's ever on the verge of landing.
It's not a path that takes you very far.
It only brings you back to where you are.

# The Berkshires

*The Appalachian ranges are believed to be
the oldest mountains in the world.*

Once jagged peaks, they're now but rolling hills,
more welcoming than when they were sublime.
The trickling water pleases where it spills,
where craggy peaks give place to rolling hills,
easing the mind like Wordsworth's daffodils.
An older mountain's easier to climb.
What once were jagged peaks are rolling hills,
more welcoming this way, if less sublime.

# A Notable Catch in a Tourist Town

Steady, as the afterdeck is shifting
beneath his boots, a fisherman is lifting
      the tuna's sickle tail
        while, hanging from the rail
    above, the cable stretches taut.
    Now, twice, the ponderous fish is caught.
Hoisted above the gathered crowd that presses,
its shadow falls on billowing sundresses
      with children under sail,
      and gulls screech overhead.
Not everyone's convinced the fish is dead.

Dwarfed by his catch, the captain's standing proudly
to one side. Choirs of tight-leashed Shih Tzus loudly
      acclaim his mighty deed.
      So many mouths to feed!
    Fashioned out of onionskin,
    the origami dorsal fin
already is a picnic spread for midges.
How creaturely is food outside of fridges;
      breathless, it still can bleed
      and may be photographed
by lovers leaning from their pleasure craft.

Even aboard the emerald yacht from Britain,
*The News*, this headline not yet even written
  has its readers hooked;
  they leave the berths they've booked
 to ask "Who? What? Where? When?" and "Why?"
  Potbellied clouds ascend the sky
and pause there, peering over someone's shoulder.
Ripplets slap their notes into a folder.
  To see where the others looked,
  each tries a different tack;
a girl in shorts climbs on her boyfriend's back.

Undaunted, at the fringe of this commotion,
the terns swoop down and plunge into the ocean,
  rise up and wheel again,
  more purposeful than men
 who've planned for months to live at ease
 two weeks in seaside properties,
only to find the constant leisure taxing.
To join the crew at work might be relaxing.
  A boy who's maybe ten
  cuts through the crowd and thrills
to catch a glimpse inside the gaping gills.

## After the Carnival

Alive! Three ants crawl
from a piece of kettle corn
the sparrow lets fall.

# Blizzard

The snow has turned to rain. The dog takes me
outside. (Let's not pretend it's otherwise.)
The night is miserable. Then suddenly
a sheet of luminescence lights the skies,

and in the moment between darknesses,
the jagged peaks and ridges, the onyx pools
gathered in bootprints, all the world there is
under the nose of dogs who drag their fools

from here to there, seem almost worth the trip.
Another flash without a thunderclap.
The leash goes taut. I lunge ahead to grip
a sapling glowing in its icy wrap,

as nearly liquid as a frozen stream.
A slap of blown sleet interrupts the dream.

## Canuck Haiku

*Île d'Orléans*

morning in Québec
freighters on the St. Lawrence
crossing the window

.

Drouin   Thibeault   Roy
second-grade classmates
names in the cemetery

.

*la maison de nos aïeux*
the ceiling so low
dreams crammed with voices

.

neighbor's open window
this afternoon Québécois
Talking Heads tonight

.

six island churches
pressed shirts and Sunday dresses
one priest   short sermon

.

no one sits up front
the monsignor steps forward
old men bow their heads

.


steeples and silos
distant mountains   curved tin roofs
streets named for old songs

.


tide's out   pressed pastel
flowers of limestone and shale
*même Dieu se souvient*

.


thrum of cargo ship
passing   wave slosh softening
moonlight   cormorant

## Stay at Home Advisory

Pity those who live apart,
unvisited, untouched, unknown,
who've kept their distance from the start,
and much prefer to be alone.

Pity the unhealthy too,
who watch the night, who sit and brood,
who really ought to pity you,
far less adept at solitude.

Pity those in attic rooms
who seldom pull the curtains back
to peer out where the sickness looms
in search of some bright thing they lack.

But those you pity may well ask,
estranged, *Was it not ever thus?*
*Who goes outside without a mask?*
*So what is quarantine to us?*

# II

*The Man in the Middle*

## Addendum

Give to Caesar what is his,
namely, everything there is.

I see a lot of eyebrows raised.
Let's check the books. You'll be amazed.

An x. An o. A hug and kiss.
Render unto Caesar this.

Render unto Caesar that.
His the dog, his the cat.

Render up your reading time.
Render, too, your reverie.

Render up the uphill climb,
render what you hope to be.

If God is dead, does Caesar get
the flip side of the coin? You bet!

Render up. You'll never win.
The croupier will rake it in.

Caesar's arms are open wide;
your whole estate will fit inside.

# The Man in the Middle

I.

Aroused from our squalor,
we cheer and we holler—
babies in Babylon
gurgle his name!

Embracing and chanting,
we race to him panting.
Aflutter we fly to him,
moths to the flame.

The man in the middle's
a cake on the griddle.
We all want a piece of him,
he is so good.

Paraders are drumming:
our champion's coming!
We'd rise from our hospital
beds if we could.

His fame is unbounded.
He's always surrounded,
right there in the middle where
no one can see.

He's kind and he's caring.
He's reckless and daring.
He's everything anyone
dreams he might be.


2.

We're learning about him.
There's reason to doubt him:
he's of the opinion
the world isn't flat.

That's one of his ruses.
He's making excuses
for why he keeps leaning
to this side or that.

The man in the middle's
too much of a riddle.
We'd always assumed he would
be one of us.

Our confidence shaken,
we feel we've been taken.
He's not with the team. He should
get off the bus.

And sooner or later
he'll prove he's a traitor,
who had us all dreaming while
we were asleep.

We're not apt to thank him.
We'll spank him and yank him
and toss him in pieces on
top of the heap.

# Epigram for Two Voices

Might poets cozy up to autocrats?

*Who knows? Fish slime is comfort food for cats.*

It's hard to think a Caesar would prefer
that kind of pet.
                    *A toothless cat can purr.*

# Napoleon's Sword

> *"The dead don't know that they are dead . . .*
> *Napoleon is still waving his sword."*
> —Isaac Bashevis Singer

Fred and Ginger glide across the set.
Benny Goodman plays the clarinet.
Marilyn adores to be adored.
Hitchcock makes the scene in silhouette.
Napoleon is brandishing his sword.

Petrarch isn't over Laura yet.
Balzac pays the interest on his debt.
Baudelaire complains of being bored.
Proust relives a past he can't forget.
Napoleon is brandishing his sword.

Leibniz has the best view one could get.
Sartre crushes out a cigarette.
Nietzsche elevates the Overlord.
Pascal collects—or settles on—his bet.
Napoleon's still brandishing his sword.

# An Indelicate Proposal

Let us conscript an army of old men
and shake them from the napping-dream of peace;
let them rejoin the wars that never cease
and heat thin blood to simmering again.

When young men die in battle, more is lost.
By laying down their lives while they are strong
for fields they haven't harvested as long,
they pay a lesser debt at greater cost.

So let us press the elders into service.
They will be recognized and celebrated,
no longer penned inside, emasculated,
clucking like old hens, ruffled and nervous,

ready for the freezer or the fryer.
What difference if the end is ice or fire?

## Samuel Clemens

Samuel Clemens spent most of his life
   scheming to make a killing.
America gets its real work done
   in spite of itself, God willing.

# Nuclear Option

Imagine that you made a list
of everyone you ever knew
(pre-supposing that you could
remember all their names);

and picture crumpling in your fist
part of your work, a page or two
to use as kindling. Next, you would
consign the rest to flames.

What if you watched the fire grow,
observing, as your writing curled,
schoolmates, lovers, relatives
reduced to flakes of ash?

You would outstrip cruel time—too slow
to seize your memories of this world—
and witness every light that lives
extinguished in a flash.

What if included in your list
was everyone you'd ever met—
the man from Belgium on the train
obsessed with Charles de Gaulle,

the officer your puppy kissed,
the bridesmaid whose chignon got wet
as she ran tripping through the rain
(you tried to break her fall)

—with no attempt at sorting out
the pricks from those you loved the best,
and anyone you've cared about
lumped in with all the rest,

mixing with men of poison minds
the man of conscience in his cell.
Oblivion accepts all kinds.
Farewell. Farewell. Farewell.

# III

*Avatars of Appetite*

# Altogether Alive

*1) Robin*

Disguised by its familiarity,
its habitat collective memory
(near AM radio and Wonder Bread),
the robin is a bird you hardly see,
out on the lawn with Bobby Kennedy,
its breast a faded Campbell-soup-can red.


*2) Black-capped Chickadee*

This cheery, hospitable chatterbox,
who flits about with friends in little flocks
twittering all year round about what's new
—where snowmelt trickles, sightings of a fox,
or when to keep an eye out for the hawks—
gives great advice to migrants passing through.


*3) American Crow*

A crow utters hello as if it coughed.
A crow prefers the jagged to the soft.
For cherubs, clouds; for crows, a broken limb.
The crow is disinclined to stay aloft,
nor can it lift its voice to join the hymn.
Who hasn't worn this darkness? Graceless, grim.

*4) Red-winged Blackbird*

Miles of rippling grass, and who would guess
that here are parceled lots? At each address
a settler stakes his claim to half an acre—
earth, stream and sky—and not a cubit less.
Perched on a cattail, watchman, early waker,
he clings to what he fiercely would possess.


*5) Herring Gull*

Avatars of appetite, they soar
above the parking lots of Burger Kings,
or hover over party boats offshore,
ravenous for mackerel heads and gore;
a churned wake draws a turbulence of wings
and frenzied cries that translate: *More! More! More!*


*6) Saltmarsh Sparrow*

*Pst!* (a secret!) *Chip! Chip! Sputter, wheeze,
throat giggle, snorer's whistle, clink of keys* . . .
This bashful sparrow's soloing suggests
the prattle of our grandchild in her nest
of pillows. Happy those soliloquies
whose Hamlets never doubt *to be* is best!

*7) Wild Turkey*

Deep chestnut brown with purple fripperies,
dandies seeking higher elevation,
wild turkey cocks roost near the tops of trees.
This love of heights survives domestication,
but dims with each succeeding generation.
The colors too. Such is a life of ease.


*8) Bobolink*

Think Zelig. Or a Forrest Gump that flies
twelve thousand miles a year through nighttime skies.
No telling where this stylish bird will be:
in Lincoln's campaign songs of liberty,
in recipes for antebellum pies,
in Amherst, skipping church with Emily . . .


*9) Red-tailed Hawk*

Like Euclid on a limb, eyes cold and clear,
he rises from his stately perch to trace
great circles in the air and, cleaving space,
extends infinity a wide embrace—
then dives! The hawk's red shriek assaults the ear.
His vector strikes its endpoint like a spear.

*10) Snowy Owl*

Shawn Klush, world's greatest Elvis wannabe,
can trace his glitzy showman's pedigree
to candelabra-flattered Liberace—
his coat of ermine purring *Look at me*—
and to the Snowy Owl, whom paparazzi
bottleneck the island road to see.


*11) Great Blue Heron*

This striking bird that Audubon depicted
as contortionist, folded to fit
color-plate 211, looks a bit
self-conscious, like an awkward teen who'd quit
whatever box they've put her in, afflicted
with uniqueness. No escaping it.


*12) Bald Eagle*

A gray midwinter morning. A clean slate.
Perched on a floodlight pole, this magistrate
leisurely eyes the stadium for small game,
unburdened by the emblematic weight
of victory and empire, wealth and fame,
and looking pretty regal just the same.

# IV

*Playthings*

# Ballad of the Terrible Silence

Melissa's crying on the phone,
    they've lost the runt of the litter.
She watched Jim bury it today.
    Experience is bitter.

Melissa calls her mom again,
    they've got the tractor running.
Oh yes, and two more kittens died.
    The others, though, are cunning.

A week goes by. "The seed is in,"
    she says, then mentions, sighing,
"Here on the farm, I'm getting used to
    things being born and dying.

"None of the kittens survived," she adds.
    "Jim buried them down by the river.
The kitchen feels cold and empty now.
    I think of them and shiver."

Melissa shows up at the door one night,
    distraught over something or other.
Her eyes are puffed up. She's been fighting with Jim.
    "He's mean," she tells her mother.

She'd seen him fling the cat at the wall,
    but that's not what upset her.
"He claims that her claws left those marks on his arm.
    It's a lie, and I know better.

"Or maybe it's true, and maybe I'm wrong—
    I've been so terribly moody!"
She runs upstairs to her old bedroom.
    Her mom finds her knitting a bootie.

"So cute," she says. "Who's having a baby?"
    Her daughter's eyes are brimming
with hopes as yet unborn themselves,
    still brightening and dimming.

While everyone readies for what is to be,
    new kittens arrive on the farm.
Jim seems to have changed, knowing he'll be a father—
    no reason to sound the alarm.

He comes along next time she visits.
    He's cradling a mewling kitten.
He pets it and never puts it down.
    He's obviously smitten.

He carries it on his shoulder, though
    it clings precariously.
"He takes it with him everywhere;
    it helps his anxiety."

He spends the evening with some friends,
    and comes in glassy-eyed.
"Where's the kitten?" Melissa asks.
    "Oh. The kitten died."

But time moves on, and time heals all,
    and love is all-enduring,
and by the time the baby comes
    Jim shows signs of maturing.

He learns to change a diaper, knows
    to warm the baby's bottle,
and does his best to tolerate
    the bawling he'd like to throttle.

He does lose his temper now and then.
    Melissa gets a shiner.
She applies a bag of frozen peas
    at break time at the diner.

She's taken a job, three shifts a week—
    a short drive to New Briton.
She worried, though, reminding him,
    "A baby's not a kitten."

When she gets home, his friends are there,
    with needles and syringes.
She screeches, "Jim, what's going on?"
    He sees her there and cringes.

"Where's the baby? Where's the baby?"
    Desperately trying to push in,
she escapes his grasp to find the child
    silent beneath a cushion.

Kneeling to kiss the staring eyes
    of the broken doll she's found,
she presses her heart to her baby's heart,
    where there is not a sound.

# The Pastime

His face is familiar—he's here all the time—
    but no one could tell you the name
of the man in the grandstand keeping score
    at a youth-league baseball game.

In Sanford, Maine, in early June,
    they don't much care who's winning.
They're hoping the gangly kid on the mound
    can make it through this inning.

Then suddenly a Honda Accord
    comes crashing through the gate,
scattering the infielders in a panic,
    skidding toward home plate.

Revving its engine, it rounds the bases
    backwards, from third to first.
Both teams retreat behind the backstop,
    their coaches fearing the worst.

The man with the scorecard flings it aside
    and leaps from his seat in the stands,
desperate to stop the automobile
    though he's only got two hands.

He sprints to where the boys are huddled,
    breathless to intervene.
He braces himself and throws his weight
    against the rusty screen.

Circling again, the driver swings wide,
    gouging the outfield grass
and picking up speed as she charges again,
    pressing her foot on the gas.

She hits the backstop at full speed.
    Flesh and metal meet,
tearing his body from its soul
    and throwing it thirty feet.

The local papers hail the man
    as a hero and a savior.
They say he fought bravely in Vietnam,
    which explains his selfless behavior.

The next day's headlines tell us more
    about the hero's past,
and where the sun had climbed so high,
    the sky is overcast.

In '68, a four-year-old died
    in a hit-and-run accident.
It was Halloween night. The driver fled.
    Nobody knew where he went.

Till five years ago. When he'd been assured
    that, given the passage of time,
he couldn't be tried for leaving the scene,
    our hero confessed to the crime.

That's when he moved to the neighboring town.
    He's lived incognito since then.
He buried his past and kept to himself,
    no different from other men.

But people unable to understand
    are prone to speculation.
The maddened woman behind the wheel—
    there must be some relation?

She must have mourned the girl who died
    a half century ago.
Was she a family friend, a neighbor?
    The young girl's sister? No.

Fate sits cross-legged, like a child
    who sets up a cardboard town,
placing figures here and there,
    only to knock them down.

# Ballad of the Dapper Black Man

A hippy chick offered to share her wine
    at the bus stop outside the casino.
We sat on her luggage, feeling free,
    slugging back the cheap vino.

A dapper black man joined us there,
    as slick as a silver spoon,
with a purple streak where his hair was parted
    and fingernails painted maroon.

"I like your attitude," he said,
    eyeing the bottle of wine.
"You've got an independent streak—
    you may have noticed mine.

"I'm not supposed to leave this town,
    because I'm on parole.
If I get caught, I lose my 'freedom.'
    If I stay, I lose my soul.

"The walls are closing in on me,
    can't take another day.
My parole officer's in bed with my Thelma.
    I got to get away."

We stood up then to wait in line;
    we all got on the bus.
The black man sat in one of the seats
    across the aisle from us.

He left my new friend his window seat
    as space for her two guitars.
We rolled out on the interstate
    under the moon and stars.

"The system owes me fifteen years.
    I spent them on death row.
My day of execution came.
    It was my time to go.

"They get you ready, set to die.
    they shave off all your hair.
I was holding a newspaper
    as I sat in the barber's chair.

"My hands shook like you wouldn't believe,
    the columns of newsprint swirled.
There was nothing in there to int'rest a man
    about to leave this world.

"Then word arrived from the governor.
    Who could believe it was real?"
He unfolded the letter so we could see
    the signature and seal.

"I hated for anyone to see
    the things I felt inside,
but I leapt up on the warden's desk,
    I crouched in the corner and cried.

"I felt just like an animal
    they let out of its cage.
I screamed for joy at the top of my lungs.
    I swore out loud in rage."

The girl beside me started to cry.
    She pleaded, "But you're free!
Get off this bus and turn around—
    you can start a new life, don't you see?

"What if they track you down?" she asked.
    He stared at his blue suede shoes.
"They will," he said. "Tomorrow night,
    they'll show me on the news."

"Cause I messed up that P.O.'s face.
    He's sleeping like the dead,
but when he blinks awake, he'll find
    Thelma tied to the bed.

"That's why I got myself fixed up—
    new threads and a manicure,
and this hairstyle I'm calling my violet streak
    will make an impression, I'm sure.

"You'll probably still be on the bus,
    so you won't be watching TV,
but everybody else—and Thelma—
    it's the last they'll see of me."

When we pulled into our next stop,
    the lights were flashing blue.
The dapper black man waved goodbye,
    "Have a good life, you two."

# The Ghost in the Cathedral

I am that daughter of The Church
    of The Holy Trinity
known as "the nun who lost a child."
    I walk the balcony

cloaked in my habit's heavy folds
    and cannot—will not—rest
as long as moldering silence holds
    the child torn from my breast.

Once having watched the flower of my heart
    shut inside the grave,
I counted my soul the smallest part
    of what I could not save—

a single one of her wrinkled toes
    I held of equal worth.
Those feet, her little ears and nose . . .
    Three shovelsful of earth!

# V

*A Sheet of Steel, a Blanket of Moss*

# Ordinary Time

We're in the waiting room. (A metaphor?
Yes, I suppose it's one you can't escape.)
Fiddling with nothing. Church-like silences.
An inwardness, eyes fixed on empty space.
There is a box of books here for the taking;
the doctor must be weeding out his shelves.
*Audubon* magazine and Solzhenitsyn . . .
The musings of forgotten naturalists,

and college textbooks I don't bother with . . .
Reticent titles, mostly. Nothing recent.
*The New Physics*, the poems of Al Zolynas.
My wife's neurologist reads poetry?
Pages here and there are folded back
to mark the poems that talk about our bodies.
"At the precise moment of death," I read,
"the pupil of the eye / opens its widest."

Only a test and followup, but I think
she wants to run away. What she went through
and put behind her looms ahead—a yawning,
unlit tunnel. She'll do an end-around:
she won't go there again. She'll grab whatever
money she can get and spend it now.
She'll buy a yacht and sail it to a villa—
buy an island with a Mastercard.

But it's our turn; the doctor leads us to
his office, not much bigger than a closet.
Encircled by his boxes full of files,
braced against the digital advance,
he's able to find her papers in an instant.
(I'm only here because I am afraid
she won't hear half of what he says to her.
She'll be away somewhere. That's why I'm here.)

A kindly, crooked smile. Age-spotted brow.
His left eye wanders slightly to one side,
softening his focus on the girl
beside me, only recently a woman
in the waiting room. The girl he knew.
Was it twenty years ago? Yes, yes.
He seems surprised to be reminded
that time does what it does. That she's alive,

that he can take some credit there, and that
she doesn't seem to mind, rather enjoys
hearing his pride expressed so like a boy's . . .
All that makes him relax into himself;
he's talking off the cuff: "To think you could
survive a thing that size inside the brain!"
*Her* brain, of course. "What size is that?" she asks.
He stops to think. "Couple of radishes."

Which she gets wrong, of course, when in the car
on our way home repeating what he said,
she mentions turnips. "Turnips?! Ah ha ha!
It's *radishes*! Can you imagine how
you'd look if you had turnips in your head?!"
Laughing like idiots on our way home.
"You see, that's why I had to come along."
Also, because, suppose she needed me . . .

# Poemmakers

Like chambermaids, we labor in obscurity,
our dreams as stale as the delivery man's.
A lack of readership can feel like purity.
We tweak the grocery list until it scans,

or count the cars that pass, as Bashō would.
We muse about the parking space not taken;
we like to see the local kid make good;
we keep the faith where it will not be shaken.

This isn't really rocket science, is it,
only a hobby a certain type enjoys.
We don't invite the epic muse to visit.
Heroic figures make a lot of noise.

Who needs another Iliad? Not me.
That sort of thing plays better on TV.

# Merry-Go-Round

> *A piece of playground equipment consisting*
> *of a small circular platform that revolves*
> *when pushed or pedaled.*
> —American Heritage Dictionary

"Here comes The Hobo!" someone said.
It was a hungry-looking clown
who wore a give-me-something frown,
his nose a stewed-tomato red,
his painted lips, blood-sausage brown.

Then clouds were whirling round a sky
some giant used a tree to stir.
My parents' faces all a blur,
I kept on waving them goodbye,
not really knowing where they were.

"Stop!" my father hollered. "Sir!"
On every face—behind a smudge
of caramel or melted fudge—
two eyes bugged out. "Get off of her!"
The drunken hobo didn't budge.

My father dragged him off the ride
growling that he'd break his teeth.
My little sister couldn't breathe.
Those kids all took the hobo's side
against the girl pressed underneath.

# House Hunters International

She was from Bulgaria, originally.
He was from Canada, not a place
where *House Hunters* would likely film a show.
In Bolivia now, they started out

by visiting a soothsayer, who read
the coca leaves he scattered round a cloth,
observing how they landed, right-side up
or upside down, and finding meaning there.

The young man kept repeating things
he heard the fortune-teller say to him,
as though he had to translate for his girlfriend.
In fact she understood as well as he did:

conveniently, the shaman spoke in English.
"He says we're going to meet with obstacles,"
he told her, and she nodded, as that is
exactly what she'd heard the shaman say.

Turns out that her Bulgarian connection
figured in the television script.
The furnishings in one place they considered
included a bright orange couch, and

other orange things which I forget,
which made the woman recollect a song
she used to sing when she was a young girl.
She sang it, "The Bulgarian Orange Song."

Did you know the Bulgarian word for orange
is orange? So that wouldn't be an obstacle. . . .
.

It must have been the song. Or after, when
the camera caught her lost in thought, off guard;
she wished, instead of flitting here and there,
they'd settle on a place to stay awhile.

Shame on me for getting teary-eyed
for people hardly different from myself—
only a couple shopping for a home,
not refugees. No one had turned them back.

They were not exiles. Neither were they moths
fluttering against the glass pane of a window,
attracted to the orange light inside,
flecks of their wings descending to the pavement.

And if they were, what would I do but watch?
The way I watch this television show,
sentimental, blurring the distinctions,
as if the Earth were one big fuzzy ball,

and I were on the inside, looking out,
the clicker there beside me on the couch.

# The Surface

> *"Le néant hante l'être."*
> —Jean-Paul Sartre

There is an emptiness in everything,
like the shade cradled in the crescent moon.

A motorcycle's engine, echoing
the large abstraction of an afternoon;

the broken gate that opens on a square,
the bricks and shadows rubbing elbows there
where silence lectures in its monotone;

another shade that walks the streets alone,
past windows—yes, the windows too are blank,
where people dwell inside their separate lives,
huddling there like money in the bank—
to where the river sheathes its glinting knives.

The tides have seized; the stillness is unreal.
The surface poses as a sheet of steel.

# Archipelago of Syllables

red keeled white boat floats
in the sky above the bay—
homemade weathervane

.

kids crying out there
on the island turn into
gulls and fly away

.

the Creator made
the jellyfish long before
Leviathan

.

peering back through my
binoculars   a gray seal's
cavernous black eyes

.

a blanket of moss
covers everything   I should
lie down and keep still

.

I hope I don't dream
of vacuum accessories
all night long   again

.

it's a long story
every stone along the shore
an eon or more

.

the great Bald Eagle
looks small in its sprawling nest
on top of the bridge

.

it gets cold   evenings
telling yourself it's summer
doesn't work for long

.

teens doing donuts
on the island's two main roads
lay some rubber down

.

seems natural that
faded plastic flamingos
poke around these weeds

.


no rush to repair
the houses whose roofs cave in
jamming their doorways

.


navigators know
these isles   like stars in the sky
are not all the same

.


admirals and monarchs
sail along these shorelines   edged
with flowering milkweed

# The Workshop

*for David Berman*


Not every second Saturday,
for sometimes you'd be traveling
abroad, or work kept you away,
but ten months out of twelve you'd bring

a bull's-eye-central metaphor,
already flawless, to present
for our critique, having made sure
to say precisely what you meant.

How easily we might misread
your absence here today. At court,
with one more major case to plead?
At anchor in a foreign port,

where you've uncorked a vintage wine?
You would have joined us otherwise;
we'd quibble with your closing line.
But this is one you won't revise.

# A Notion

Up in the middle of the night again,
remembering things of no significance—
the mice that shared the cellar of our place
out in the Berkshires those two summers, rain
cascading through one wall of the foundation,
cobwebs hanging thick as Spanish moss . . .
—I wonder, will the spirit absently
recall the flesh that housed it for a time?

# VI

*Old Brick Church*

# Tell You the Story

It was all over
the news. My son's friend
stabbed a professor
twenty-seven times
with a painting knife
in the school bathroom.
His father, Doctor
So-and-So, wouldn't
allow a shrink to
testify in court—
what would people think?
The friend went to jail
for being sane while
stabbing.

      Years later,
released, took a job
moving gravel with
heavy machinery,
wound up crushed beneath
two tons, losing both
legs. In a wheelchair,
began to project
Satanic visions
on the world outside,
implicating those
few friends left to him
in a cosmic plot
to drag him under.

He sent recorded
messages threatening
to take revenge on
those traitors and rats
who might expose him
to the police for
thinking evil thoughts.
His mother a witch.
My son's, another.
And the old lady
next door—whom he watched
from his immobile
vantage—schemed against
his life.

    He wielded
demonic power
to protect himself
from the medicine
forced on him. Those who
hadn't quit caring
desperately looked
for ways to help him.
The police refused
to get involved till
given *evidence*
of homicidal
tendencies.

My son,
who brings the Bible
with him everywhere
(crazy, right?), stayed loyal.
He refused to forward
to the state police
the texts his troubled
friend kept sending him—
threatening to bash
his face in—to which
he'd always respond:

*Love you brother. You
should trust your mother.
Please accept the help
you need. May God be
with you.*
               *Your friend,* \_\_\_\_.
That brought in reply
another screed growled
in the devil's voice.

At the old brick church
in Saint Johnsbury,
I knelt with my son,
who struggled to keep
himself physically
still, questioning if
he'd mistaken his own
code of honor for
the Lord's will.

                    He left
the building shaken
when Mass ended, found
where he parked his truck
and saw the message
on his phone. It read:
"He's in the psych ward."

An answer of sorts.

# An Irreverent Portrait of Father McLaughlin

> *"Christians were never meant to be normal."*
> —Jacques Ellul

Cheers to Father McLaughlin, master of
the convoluted anecdote, who's known
to interrupt himself mid-sermon to
explore an etymology—the Bugs
Bunny of liturgists, whose faith alone
brings order to his spirit's messy room,
where he can hang his hat on *God is Love*.
That's all his ministry, three words. And hugs.
Against the Catholic preference for doom,
three words for all that's beautiful and true.
It leaves a priest with little else to say.
He talks a mile a minute anyway,

citing the authors of the books he reads
and gives to friends, then buys to read again.
(Their heady absinthe makes the heart grow fonder.)
There's Heaney's verse, and Vendler's commentary,
Yves Congar's writings from the Vatican—
a journal of eleven hundred pages!
He strings together quotes like rosary beads
—Welty, Dickinson, the dictionary....
The bookstore gets a quarter of his wages
for earthly treasures he is quick to squander.
Avarice feeds his generosity.
Of all those words, he clings to only three.

Once, when the faithful turned eyes inward so
the ears still left to hear were hardly any,
he paused before the phrase, *The Mass is ended*,
and said he had a cryptic message for us.
(Was I alone in thinking one of many?)
"U. A. Fanthorpe's in the vestibule."
Another utterance ex nihilo
that no one tried to understand. The chorus
sang, we buttoned up, the air turned cool
then cold as the church doors swung wide; we wended
our slow ways through pews and down the aisle.
He met me with a package and a smile.

It was a book of poems. I recognized
the author's name as one I'd heard but once:
just now. The cryptic message was for me!
I laughed aloud, without quite knowing why.
Although my friend would rather play the dunce
than stand on ceremony with his friends,
an in-joke from the altar? Ill-advised.
But who was there to give advice? Not I.
I felt like I'd been drifting at loose ends,
puzzling over nothings recently,
overwhelmed by every simple thing
that baffled my inept deciphering.

In spite of—or because of—that cracked cup
of nonsense stirred with Charity, I guess
no tea could better help me clear my head.
This Fanthorpe's quite a poet, too: *in touch
with the sustaining ordinariness
of things.* Even in cafeterias,
the plates and saucers, always looking up.
Let skeptics diss religion as 'a crutch'—
McLaughlin takes a stand, that's what he does.
Three words. And yes, the breaking of the bread.
It's no man's code; it's not the Golden Rule.
Who would be wise, let him become a fool.

# Wretched Rocco

> *And they were astonished out of measure,*
> *saying among themselves, who then can be*
> *saved? And Jesus looking upon them saith,*
> *with men it is impossible . . .*
> —Mark 10:26-27a

There'll be no place for you, pesky Rocco.
They'll lose all trace of you, nudgy Rocco.
Too many angels on a pin—
they won't be squeezing tomcats in.
There'll be no place for you, nudgy Rocco.
They'll want to fold their wings and rest;
you're an unwelcome little pest.
There'll be no place for you, nudgy Rocco.

No scratching at the gate, prowling Rocco.
No snatching from the plate, slinking Rocco.
Saint Pete will shout out, "Nothing doin'!"
He'll direct you to your ruin.
No scratching at the gate, clawing Rocco.
Don't wail and claim you're innocent;
you'll wake Elijah in his tent.
No scratching at the gate, prowling Rocco.

You'll fast while others feast, thieving Rocco.
The last shall be the least, sneaky Rocco.
In the land of milk and honey,
naughty cats will not get any.
You'll fast while others feast, thieving Rocco.
When the blessed wine is poured
you'll get to lick a dried-out gourd;
you'll fast while they all feast, thieving Rocco.

No miracle of fish, whiny Rocco.
No mackerel on your dish, griping Rocco.
As the Saints go marching in
they'll toss your way an empty tin.
No miracle of fish, irksome Rocco.
There'll be no scrap that you can ferret
in the world the meek inherit.
No miracle of fish, irksome Rocco.

We get what we deserve, wicked Rocco.
You've got a lot of nerve, wicked Rocco.
While saints are singing in the light
you'll still be howling in the night;
you'll get what you deserve, wicked Rocco.
Don't think that it'll be a lark
because you've always loved the dark.
We get what we deserve, wicked Rocco.

Don't look to me for pity, wretched Rocco.
I'm not on the committee, wretched Rocco.
When the omniscient Judge has tried you
don't depend on me to hide you;
don't look to me for pity, wretched Rocco.
You've witnessed how I choose to live
and things the bishops won't forgive;
don't look to *me* for pity, wretched Rocco.

You'll share the misery, wretched Rocco.
Beware of what's to be, wretched Rocco.
Your crime was being born a cat.
The fitting punishment for that?
Eternal misery, wretched Rocco.
Although your fault's no greater than
my fault of being born a man . . .
we'll share the misery, wretched Rocco.

We'll have to pay for our mistakes.
Let's see how long forever takes.
Forever. You and me, wretched Rocco.

# His Eyes Rest on Julia, Sleeping

> *"Tis Julia's bed, and she sleeps there."*
> —Robert Herrick

To themselves, the olive, fig and grape
are cargoes tight-sealed in their darkened holds.
No matter if its tang is brassy-bright,
the tangerine is tongueless in its sphere.

Likewise, the hollowed stone that cups the rain
can't know its coolness on the wrist or nape.
The willow's shade does nothing for the willow.
The stars don't preen themselves when skies are clear,

nor is the cherry blossom given sight.
The trickling stream is silent to itself.
All music's owed to love, that wakes the senses;
those strings are mute that none can ever hear.

So love, that turned this world and gave it shape,
has need that I should keep watch through the night.

# Talking All Night

*for RPE*

I asked my friend, the poet,
how she was getting by.
"Work and tears,"
came her reply.

"And listening," she added,
"in silence, to be sure.
I listen closer
now than before.

It is a lot like reading,
a thing I loved to do . . .
What book felt like
first love to you?"

"It was in French," I said,
"a book my mother kept
to read to us
until we slept.

Not a children's book—
an excerpt from Hugo?
or Maupassant . . .
with etchings, though,

in which, from room to room,
as gentle as a mouse,
the family bear
wandered the house.

The bear saw everything,
and knew their secrets well,
but couldn't speak,
so couldn't tell.

The grateful children fed him
Crêpes Suzette and tarts;
for his mute love
had warmed their hearts.

I thrilled to see that book
in the case beside my bed,
to hear, again,
things left unsaid.

And I'd imagine what
the bear kept to himself—
stories to fill
another shelf!"

Although my tale continued
longer than it should,
my friend's clear eyes
pronounced it good;

as in a dream that takes
for granted the absurd,
she'd understood
my every word.

Long will I remember,
if memory is kind,
how warm she made
those rooms of mind.

# Gibbous Moon

Unheralded, the gibbous moon
arrives too late, if not too soon,
a goblet neither full nor empty,
off balance there, like Humpty Dumpty
or one of us, afraid of falling,
having missed a stair or calling,

lopped mushroom cap, a thing diminished,
or handwork set aside unfinished,
a doily of discolored lace
moth-eaten in an attic space,
age-spotted face obscurely seen
peering through a storm door screen,

ragged moon in a ragged cloud,
Lazarus risen, trailing his shroud,
a powdered thumbprint on the sky
that blurs the stars we travel by,
thin wafer vagrant souls are fed,
wholly insufficient bread

we bless and break, and multiply.

# Acknowledgments

My thanks to the following publications, where several of the poems in this manuscript first appeared or are scheduled to appear:

*Able Muse:* "Canuck Haiku"

*America:* "Gibbous Moon"

*Asses of Parnassus:* "Epigram for Two Voices"

*Beltway Poetry Quarterly:* "Napoleon's Sword"

*Crosswinds Poetry Journal:* "Ordinary Time"

*First Things:* "Addendum" and "Talking All Night"

*Ibbetson Street:* "Archipelago of Syllables"

    "After the Carnival"

    "Ballad of the Dapper Black Man"

    "Ballad of the Terrible Silence"

    "The Ghost in the Cathedral"

    "Merry-go-round"

    "The Pastime"

    "Poemmakers"

*Literary Matters:* "Tell You the Story"

*Merrimac Mic Anthology:* "Samuel Clemens"

*Modern Age:* "A Notable Catch in a Tourist Town" and "The Workshop"

*Montreal Review:* "Altogether Alive"

*New England Poetry Club (website):* "An Indelicate Proposal"

*New Verse Review:* "Wretched Rocco"

*Plough:* "The Berkshires" and "The Path"

*Presence:* "An Irreverent Portrait of Father McLaughlin"

*Pulsebeat Poetry Journal:* "The Man in the Middle"

*Think:* "His Eyes Rest on Julia, Sleeping"

*Valparaiso Poetry Review:* "Blizzard"

*What Rough Beast:* "Stay at Home Advisory"

"Altogether Alive" was commissioned by David Yang, director of the Newburyport Chamber Music Festival, for performance in August 2024.

"Addendum" was included in Scribner's *The Best American Poetry 2018*.

An earlier version of "House Hunters International" appeared in *LEON* as "People Out There in the World."

An earlier version of "The Surface" appeared in *What Rough Beast* as "Shelter in Place."

# About the Poet

ALFRED NICOL, who worked in the printing industry for over twenty years after graduating from Dartmouth College, published his first book of poems, *Winter Light*, in 2004. His other publications include *Animal Psalms*, *Elegy for Everyone*, and *Brief Accident of Light*, a collaboration with Rhina P. Espaillat. Nicol's translation of *One Hundred Visions of War* by Julien Vocance has been called "an essential addition to the history of modernist poetry." His poems have appeared in *Poetry*, *The New England Review*, *Dark Horse*, *Commonweal*, *The Formalist*, *The Hopkins Review*, and in many anthologies including *The Best American Poetry 2018* and *Contemporary Catholic Poetry*. His translation of the lyrics to "Győzelemről énekeljen" were used for the official anthem of the 52nd International Eucharistic Congress convened in 2021 by Pope Francis in Budapest. As part of the music-and-poetry ensemble, The Diminished Prophets, Nicol has performed melopoeia for over twenty years with Espaillat and classical/flamenco guitarist John Tavano. In recent years, the Newburyport Chamber Music Festival has commissioned several works of poetry for its annual event. Nicol lives in Massachusetts with his wife, the artist Gina DiGiovanni.

# About Wiseblood Books

If you loved this book, we know you will enjoy other titles from the Wiseblood Books catalog. There, you will find fiction, poetry, and monographs from many of America's most talented and promising literary writers including Dana Gioia, Marly Youmans, Sally Thomas, Alfred Nicol, Rhina P. Espaillat, James Matthew Wilson, J. C. Scharl, Katy Carl, Dan Rattelle, and many more. In supporting this hardworking independent press, and the talented authors who publish through it, you will be participating in the good work of promoting new literature and our mission to foster works of fiction, poetry, and philosophy that wrestle us from the ruse of distraction; find redemption in uncanny places and people; articulate faith and doubt in their incarnate complexity; dare an unflinching gaze at human beings as "political animals"; and render well this world's sufferings without forfeiting hope—all of this with wide-eyes.

Review our catalog and purchase directly at www.wisebloodbooks.com, or request a copy of any of our books from your favorite bookseller.

You can also help other readers find this book, by giving a copy to a friend, suggesting it for a reading group, requesting the title for your local library, sharing your response via social media, or by writing and publishing a review.

We are grateful for your support in building a rich culture of contemporary literature.

www.ingramcontent.com/pod-product-compliance
Lightning Source LLC
Chambersburg PA
CBHW070157080526
44586CB00015B/2023